CITIES THROUGH TIME

Los Angeles

A photographic exploration of how the
city has developed and changed

ANNE ROONEY

Chrysalis Children's Books

First published in the UK in 2005 by
Chrysalis Children's Books
An imprint of Chrysalis Books Group Plc
The Chrysalis Building, Bramley Road,
London W10 6SP

ISBN 1 84458 354 6

British Library Cataloguing in Publication Data for this book
is available from the British Library.

Anne Rooney has asserted her right under the Copyright,
Design and Patents Act 1988 to be identified as the
author of this work.

Contact Anne Rooney by e-mail (anne@annerooney.co.uk)
or visit her website (www.annerooney.co.uk).

Associate Publisher Joyce Bentley
Editorial Manager Rasha Elsaeed
Project Editor Leon Gray
Editorial Assistant Camilla Lloyd
Consultant Jeff Lewis
Designer Alix Wood
Illustrator Mark Walker
Picture Researcher Jamie Dikomite

Printed in China

10 9 8 7 6 5 4 3 2 1

Read Regular, READ SMALLCAPS and Read Space;
European Community Design Registration 2003
and Copyright © Natascha Frensch 2001-2004
Read Medium, **Read Black** and *Read Slanted*
Copyright © Natascha Frensch 2003-2004

READ™ is a revolutionary new typeface that will
enhance children's understanding through clear, easily
recognisable character shapes. With its evenly spaced
and carefully designed characters, READ™ will help
children at all stages to improve their literacy skills,
and is ideal for young readers, reluctant readers
and especially children with dyslexia.

Picture Acknowledgments
All reasonable efforts have been made to ensure the
reproduction of content has been done with the consent
of copyright owners. If you are aware of any unintentional
omissions please contact the publishers directly so that any
necessary corrections may be made for future editions.

T=Top, B=Bottom, L=Left, R=Right, C=Centre
The Bruce Torrence Hollywood Historical Collection: FC B, 8,
16, 17T, 18T, 22, 24B
California Historical Society, Title Insurance and Trust Photo
Collection, Department of Special Collections, University of
Southern California: FC TL, BC TL, 6, 10T, 14, 18B, 20, 24T,
26, 28
Corbis: 3, 7 C. Moore
David Rumsey Map Collection, www.davidrumsey.com: 5R
Getty Images: 15T Deborah Davis
Hearst Newspaper Collection, Department of Special
Collections, University of Southern California: 10B
Rex Features/Everett Collection: BC C, 4
Science Photo Library: 5L CNES, 1994 DISTRIBUTION SPOT
IMAGE
Simon Clay/Chrysalis Image Library: FC TR, FC C, BC TR, 1, 2,
9, 11, 13, 15B, 17B, 19, 21, 23, 25, 27, 29, 31
Whittington Collection, Department of Special Collections,
University of Southern California: 12

CONTENTS

In less than a hundred years, Los Angeles has grown from a small farming community into one of the largest cities in the USA. Los Angeles is most famous for Hollywood – the heart of the world's movie industry and the home of many great film stars.

Then and now

Los Angeles was founded as a Spanish settlement in 1781 by Governor Felipe de Neve, who brought Mexican settlers into the area. Los Angeles made money first from farming, then from the Gold Rush and finally from the film industry. The city has attracted millions of people hoping to make a fortune or just enjoy a better life in a warm climate. Los Angeles is on the Pacific Coast of North America. It is the second largest city in the USA, with a population of more than 3.8 million people. The history of Los Angeles is marked by the tension between the USA and its neighbour Mexico. The city has also seen some of the world's most destructive earthquakes.

A girl meets characters at Disneyland, 1960

Time line

8,000 BCE Native Americans first settle in the area

1781 Eleven families of settlers arrive and found 'The Town of the Queen of the Angels'

1818 First American, English-speaking person settles in Los Angeles after being shipwrecked as a pirate

1842 Discovery of gold precipitates the California Gold Rush

1542 First Europeans make contact with Native Americans in the region

1804 First orange grove planted in Los Angeles

1819 Death of Manuel Camero – the last of the original settlers

1847 Mexico defeated in last stand against Americans occupying California

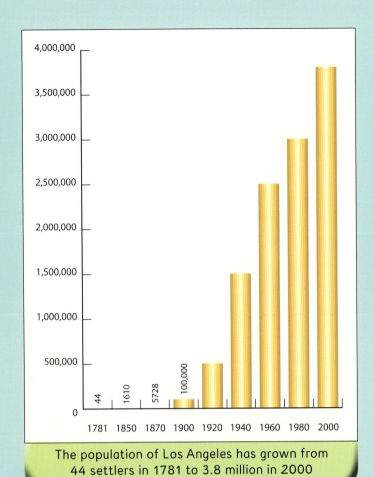

The population of Los Angeles has grown from 44 settlers in 1781 to 3.8 million in 2000

How to use this book

In this book you will find photos of Los Angeles as it was in the past and as it is now. There are questions about the photos to get you to look at and think about them carefully. You may need to do some research to answer some of the questions. You might be able to use:

- encyclopaedias
- CD-ROMs
- reference books
- the Internet.

Page 30 lists useful websites and some films you might like to watch, which show Los Angeles at different times.

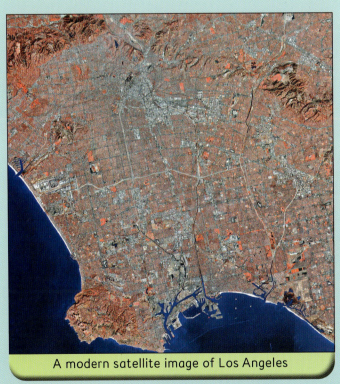

A modern satellite image of Los Angeles

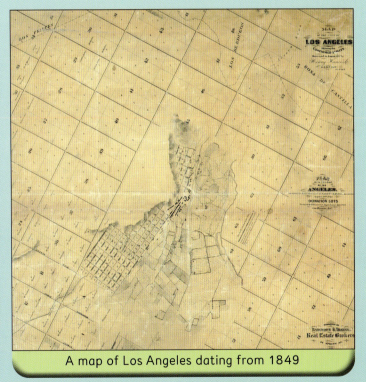

A map of Los Angeles dating from 1849

1861 Los Angeles divided by the American Civil War

1869 The world's first transcontinental railway links the East and West coasts of the USA; it reaches Los Angeles in 1876

1887 Work starts on the construction of Hollywood

1950s Severe air pollution kills many people

1861–1862 Flooding and severe drought kill most livestock in Los Angeles and end cattle farming in the area

1871 Mass attack on Chinese people following trouble in Chinatown; 30 people die

1909 First Hollywood film completed

1992 Race riots cause 58 deaths and millions of dollars worth of damage

Hollywood is the heart of the movie industry. It was built in the northwest part of Los Angeles when the owner of the land sold it for development in the 1880s. Today, many film stars have made their homes in nearby Beverly Hills. These two photos show how this part of the city has changed in the last 70 years.

Back in time

- What differences can you spot in the two photos of Hollywood?
- How are the buildings different?
- Many new buildings have been built in Los Angeles in the last few years. What do you think these buildings are being used for?

- Imagine you are in Hollywood in the 1930s. How do you think it would feel different compared with today?
- What are the open spaces in the recent photo being used for? Can you find similar open spaces in the old photo?

Hollywood panorama, 1930s

Rapid development

Hollywood was created on land owned by a rancher called Harvey Wilcox. In just a few decades, Hollywood grew from orange groves and bean fields into a thriving city – famous as the home of the movie industry. However, not all cities grow so quickly. Many take hundreds of years to develop.

- What would you expect to find in a city that developed slowly over hundreds of years?
- How would this city differ from a city such as Los Angeles that developed very quickly?
- Find out about the town or city nearest to you, or that you live in. Is it old or new? Look at the streets and buildings. When were they built, and how did the city grow?
- Is your town or city famous for anything? If so, what?

Investigate

Find out about a new town and an old town near where you live. What are they like? How are they different? Make a wall chart with pictures and maps, pointing out some of the things that you can find in both towns. What types of buildings are found in the old town? Are they different from buildings in the new town?

Hollywood panorama

Originally, the Cahuenga Pass was a Native American footpath and burial ground. Later, it was used by Spanish and Mexican herders, who drove their cattle across the mountains. Today, a busy motorway has been built at Cahuenga Pass, carrying traffic into Los Angeles.

Mascarel Ranch, 1896

Ranch to road

Joe Mascarel was a French sea captain who came to Los Angeles from Mexico in 1844. In the late 19th century, he built a ranch, which became a successful farm. As Los Angeles grew, Mascarel gave up farming and built expensive houses on his land. These houses have since been demolished. The area now has apartments, commercial buildings and cheap motels.

- What is the tall structure on the right of the old photo of Mascarel's Ranch?
- Many people in the old photo do not look dressed for farm work. Who do you think they are? Which of these people might work on the land?
- What vehicles can you see in the old photo of the Cahuenga Pass? What were they used for?
- What vehicles can you see in the recent photos?

Cahuenga Pass, 1889

Growing city

Los Angeles has been transformed from farmland into a busy city that is the home of a glamorous and wealthy industry. As more people settle in a new city, the surrounding area is converted from countryside into places where people can live. Sometimes, forest is cut down or swamp land drained so that the houses can be built.

- Do you think the same type of people live in Los Angeles now as lived there a hundred years ago?
- Why do you think the motorway was built?
- What effect might this have had on local wildlife?

Gower Street, site of Mascarel Ranch

Investigate

Cities often grow up near rivers or the sea, where people can travel easily for trade. Other cities are built near a valuable natural resource, such as a coal or oil deposit, because people can use it or sell it.

Find out about the history of your own town, city or village. What attracted people to settle down in the area? Make a booklet about the place where you live, showing what the land has been used for and how it has changed.

Hollywood Freeway at Cahuenga Pass

The Biltmore Hotel opened in 1923. The hotel has been refurbished many times, most notably in 1984, when it was renamed the Regal Biltmore Hotel. Angel's Flight railway opened in 1901. The line was taken out of service in the 1960s but restored and reopened in 1996. It was closed after an accident in 2001.

Angel's Flight railway, early 19th century

Building up

- What is the most obvious difference in each of the two places shown on these pages?
- What is the tallest building in each of the old photos and each of the new photos?
- How do the new buildings look different from the old buildings?
- Why do you think the new buildings are so tall?

The Biltmore Hotel, 1920s–30s

Fitting in

When architects plan new buildings, they usually try to make them fit in with their surroundings. We do not see a building on its own – we always see it in its surroundings.

- Is there somewhere in your local area where old and new buildings are side by side?
- Are the new buildings built from the same sort of materials as the older buildings?
- Try to imagine how the old buildings might have looked when they were first built. Do you think they would have seemed different back then?
- How well do you think architects have planned the new buildings so that they fit in with their environment?

Angel's Flight

Investigate

Pick a place in your local area where there are old buildings and new buildings side by side. Imagine that you live or work in one of the old buildings. Write a letter to the people who have built the new building, either complaining about some of the things you do not like about it or telling them about things you do like. Say how it has changed the way your old building looks or feels.

The Regal Biltmore Hotel

The first Chinese settlers arrived in Los Angeles in the 1850s. By 1870, about two hundred Chinese people lived in an area called Chinatown. The early settlers brought their customs and traditions with them, cooking Chinese food and building their houses in traditional styles. Chinese people were forced to leave Chinatown in 1932 and move to a place called Little Italy, where many Italian people lived. A new Chinatown was built on land owned by China. It opened in 1938. Today, the area combines Chinese culture with the modern American way of life.

China city

- How does Chinatown look different from the other parts of Los Angeles shown in this book?
- Why do you think Chinatown is different?
- What differences can you spot in the two photos of Chinatown?
- Look at the photos of the Chinese Theater on pages 14 and 15. What is similar about the Chinese Theater and the buildings in Chinatown?

Chinatown, early 19th century

A popular place

Chinatown is popular with other people who live in Los Angeles, and many tourists also visit the area while they are on holiday in the city.

- Why do you think people visit Chinatown? What do you think people like to do when they go there?
- Do you think that the people living in Chinatown like having visitors? How would you feel about tourists if you lived there?
- Imagine you have moved to a different country, where people speak a different language. Do you think you would prefer to live among people from your own country? What do you think you would miss about the country from which you moved?
- Can you think of any reasons why people would want to move from one country to live in another country?

Investigate

Imagine that you have moved from China to live in Chinatown. Some of your friends and family are still in China. Draw a picture for a postcard. On the back of your postcard, describe what you like about your new home and what you do not like. Explain what is good about living in Chinatown rather than elsewhere in the city.

Chinatown

13

Los Angeles is home to many theatres that are used to show films and plays. Some of the theatres are built in exotic styles that recall the settings of the films they put on. The première (opening night) of a film is a big event, with as much spectacle and excitement as possible. The Chinese Theater opened in 1927. An actress stepped in wet cement in front of the theatre, and the owner then persuaded other movie stars to do the same. The collection of cement prints is now a tourist attraction.

Show time

- How have the Chinese Theater and its surroundings changed. How have they stayed the same?
- Do you think the inside of the Chinese Theater will have changed?
- How does the Chinese Theater look different from the theatres in your area?
- Do you think it would be different to watch a film in the Chinese Theater rather than your local cinema?

Chinese Theater, 1930

Strange styles

Architects often design buildings in a style that is unusual for the area or time, because they are attracted to the age and find it exotic.

- Can you think of a building in your local area that is designed in an unusual style? Maybe it has been made to look as if it is from a different country. Why do you think it was designed in this way? What is it used for? Do you like it?

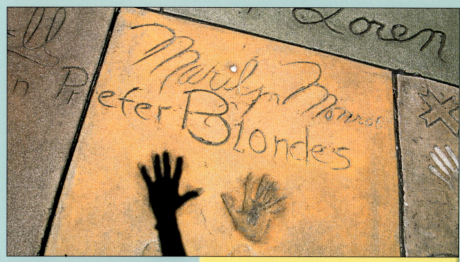

Marilyn Monroe's hand prints

Chinese Theater

The first Hollywood film studio was built twenty years after the old photo of Sunset Boulevard below was taken. Soon there were many studios, and Hollywood became the centre of the American movie industry. One of the most famous studios was the Sunset-Gower Studio, which can be seen in the photo shown on the next page.

Playing the part

Early films were shot on large sets, where the buildings and scenes were specially made for each film. The inset photo opposite shows a set made to look like ancient Babylon for the film Intolerance. Very few films are made in this way today.

- How might the families of the girls shown in the photo below have earned a living in Los Angeles in 1905?
- Look at the recent photo of Sunset Boulevard. Do you think this is a rich or a poor area now? How can you tell?
- How do you think it would have felt to be on the set of the film Intolerance in 1916?

Sunset Boulevard, 1905

Film effects

The movie industry is very important to many people who live and work in Los Angeles.

- Do you know anywhere in your local area where one type of activity is most important to the people who live and work there? Perhaps you live in an area where most people work in the tourist industry or as farmers. How does it make the area different?

- Most modern films are made using special effects created by people using computers. Think of a movie you have seen recently. How was it made? Can you tell how special effects have been used in the film? In what ways do you think the special effects made the film more enjoyable or exciting?

Investigate

Watch a film that was made at one of the old Hollywood Studios (see page 30). Can you tell if it was shot in a studio or on a set rather than in a real place? Would the film be different if it had been shot on location (in a real setting)? Write a review of the film, saying what it is about, what is good and bad about it and how you think it was made.

Inset: The Babylonian set for *Intolerance*, 1916

Sunset Boulevard at Gower

17

The Glen Holly Hotel was popular with tourists in the 1890s. The horse-drawn coaches in the early photo below took tourists on trips around the area. The Beverley Wilshire Hotel is a grand hotel that has been used by the rich and famous since it was built in 1927. It is a tourist attraction that was built as a film set in 1920 and then used as the offices of a film studio. The Witch's House had to be moved from its original site as drivers were being distracted as they drove past, causing many accidents.

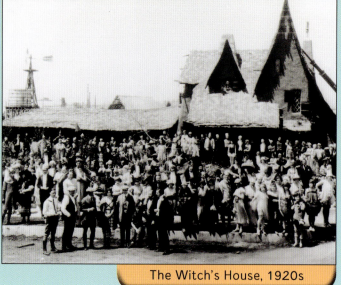

The Witch's House, 1920s

Hotels and houses

- What differences can you see in the photos of the Glen Holly Hotel and the Beverley Wilshire Hotel?
- How has The Witch's House changed? What is still the same?
- How would it be different to see Los Angeles from a horse-drawn coach rather than a modern bus or car?

Glen Holly Hotel, 1900

Tourist attractions

Many people visit Los Angeles every year. Tourists travel from other parts of America and from many countries around the world.

- What do you think people go to see when they visit Los Angeles?
- Find out about some of the tours that are put on by the major Hollywood film studios.
- What other places in Los Angeles attract tourists? Think about areas of natural beauty, such as beaches and parks, as well as purpose-built tourist attractions.
- Tourism has both advantages and disadvantages for the local area. How can tourism be good for an area? How can tourists harm the places that they visit?
- How do you think tourism affects the lives of people who live and work in Los Angeles? Can you think of some reasons why these people would like having tourists?

The Witch's House

Investigate

Using the Internet or guide books find out as much as you can about one of the main tourist attractions in Los Angeles. Make a leaflet to describe what people can do there, and explain why you think it might be worth a visit.

Beverly Wilshire Hotel

Santa Monica was a popular beach resort during the 1890s. Public swimming pools, called bathhouses, were built along the beach, and many film stars bought summer houses there. In 1911, a pier opened with roller coaster rides and many other tourist attractions, but the pier was completely wrecked by a fire in the following year. The fire destroyed all the amusements around the beach and a large area of the business district of Santa Monica.

Sands of change

- What differences can you see in the old and new photos of Santa Monica beach? Are there any things that are still the same in the new photo of Santa Monica beach?

- What are the people doing on the beach?
- What is happening in the small photo below? How does the swimwear differ from modern swimwear?

Inset: Women in their bathing suits, Santa Monica Pier

Santa Monica Beach, early 19th century

Beach life

Many people go to beaches to relax in the sun, play in the sand, swim in the sea and visit amusement arcades and piers that have been built to attract tourists.

- Is Santa Monica like beaches that you have been to or live near?
- What do you like to do when you go to the beach? Do you like to do the same things as the people you can see in these photos?

Investigate

Find out what people did at popular beach resorts in your own country at some time during the last hundred years. Do people visiting beach resorts today do similar things? What can you find out about the special foods people ate at the beach, games they played and activities they enjoyed? Where did people stay? What did they wear in the sea and on the beach?

Imagine that you live near a popular beach resort. Make a poster to attract tourists to the area. The poster should advertise some of the activities that people can do on the beach and in the surrounding area.

Santa Monica Beach with Santa Monica Pier in the background

Movie stars used to go to Schwab's Pharmacy to buy items that were difficult to find in Los Angeles, such as high-quality cosmetics. It also sold food and ice creams. Schwab's was demolished in 1988, and the Virgin Megastore you can see in the recent photo replaced it. The Hollywood Cash Grocery was built in 1886 and was Hollywood's first permanent general store. The man who delivered customers' groceries also picked up their letters and took them to the post office.

Shops and stores

- How are the buildings different in the four photos on these pages?
- What do you think you can buy in the Virgin Megastore, which has replaced Schwab's Pharmacy?
- What do you think you can buy in Jack in the Box, which has replaced the Hollywood Cash Grocery?
- Look at the signs on the Hollywood Cash Grocery. What things do they mention that you could buy? Where do people buy these things now?

Schwab's Pharmacy

Hollywood Cash Grocery, 19th century

Goods for sale

In many places, small shops have been replaced by large supermarkets. Often these supermarkets are farther away from the places where people live.

- Do people still buy goods from general stores such as Schwab's Pharmacy and the Hollywood Cash Grocery?
- Were the things that people now buy in stores such as the Virgin Megastore and Jack in the Box available a hundred years ago?
- Besides going to the shops, how else do people buy things today?
- How are the lives of people affected if local shops are replaced by big, out-of-town supermarkets?

Jack in the Box

Virgin Megastore

Investigate

Imagine that you run a small shop in the street where you live. Who would use it? What would they buy? How would you encourage people to buy goods at your shop rather than travel to a supermarket farther away? Make up an advertisement for your shop in a local newspaper or magazine. Cut out pictures of things you would sell and stick them on your poster.

The train line shown in the old photo at the bottom of this page was built in 1888. Hollywood's first railway was built in 1887. It ran through the centre of the city, but the rail tracks have now been removed. The Los Angeles Police Department (LAPD) started using bicycles instead of horses in the late 19th century. Today, private security firms help the LAPD look after the city. Some of the officers still use bicycles to patrol the streets.

LAPD on bikes, Broadway, 1904

Travelling in the city

- Is the train in the old photo like modern trains?
- Can people still ride in trains like this? If so, where?
- Look closely at the old and new photos of Hollywood Boulevard. In what ways has the area changed?
- What do you think it would have been like to live in the house behind the train in the old photo of Hollywood Boulevard?
- What do you think it would be like to live in one of the buildings on the side of Hollywood Boulevard today?
- Why do you think the police used bicycles in the 1890s? Why do the security officers use bicycles today?

Hollywood Boulevard, 1893

Transport types

Los Angeles is huge, and the city is spread out over a large area. Today, most people drive to work, school and the shops.

- Why were trains so popular in Los Angeles in the 1880s?
- Why do many people now prefer to travel in Los Angeles by car?
- What kinds of journeys do people in your local area make by car? Why?
- Do you travel by train? If so, where do you go when you use the train?
- Make a list of some of the advantages and disadvantages of travelling by train, car and bicycle.
- Different types of transport affect the environment in different ways. Which types of transport do most harm to the environment? What sort of damage do they cause?
- Which types of transport do least harm to the environment?

Investigate

Conduct a survey to find out how people in your class travel to school, to the shops and to local places, such as the swimming pool or cinema. Draw a bar chart from the results of your survey. Are there any alternatives to the types of transport your classmates use? Could they use public transport or walk for some of the journeys they make by car?

Security officers on bikes, Broadway

Hollywood Boulevard

Originally, the Otis Art Institute was a private house. When the owner died, he bequeathed it to the city of Los Angeles, which turned it into an art institute. The original Otis Art Institute building burned down in 1920, and a new building replaced it. Eventually, the institute grew too big, and so it moved to a new location in Santa Monica. The original Shrine Auditorium also burned down in 1920. Six years later, it was replaced with a building that is protected against fire and earthquake damage. Today, it is used for shows, awards ceremonies and grand dinners.

Otis Art Institute, early 20th century

Art houses

- What differences and similarities can you see in the two photos of the Otis Art Institute?
- How do you think the old building was changed inside to convert it from a private house into an art institute?
- Is the old Shrine Auditorium like other American buildings from the early 20th century you can see in this book?
- What similarities can you see in the two photos of the Shrine Auditorium?

Shrine Auditorium, 1910

Fire damage

In both of the examples on these pages, the original buildings were destroyed by fire. New buildings were put up to serve the same purposes. Sometimes an old building is demolished deliberately and another put in its place, even though it will be used in the same way.

● Why do you think this might happen? Has this happened near you? If so, how is the new building different from the old one it replaced?

Sometimes, whole areas can change. There are several examples in this book. Look at the old and recent photos of Mascarel's Ranch on pages 8 and 9 and those of Hollywood Boulevard on pages 24 and 25.

● What effects do you think major changes such as these have on the people who live in the areas?

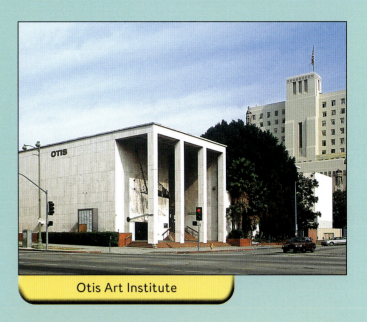
Otis Art Institute

Investigate

Find out about an area in your town or city that has changed completely in recent years. Use a tape recorder to record a programme for your local radio station. Find out how the area has changed. What was the area used for before? What is it used for now? How has the change affected people who live or work in the area?

Shrine Auditorium

Bullocks Wilshire was built as a smart shop in 1929. It is designed in a style known as Art Deco, which was very popular at the time. As shopping malls were built elsewhere across the city, Bullocks Wilshire became less popular, and eventually it closed. The building has since been restored, and it is now a law college. The Church of the Good Shepherd was built in 1923. Several famous film stars have been married or buried in the church, including Elizabeth Taylor and Rudolph Valentino.

Old and new

- Has anything changed in the old and new photos of the buildings on these two pages?
- Bullocks Wilshire is no longer used for its original purpose. Why do you think the building was restored?

- How do you think the inside of Bullocks Wilshire might have changed?
- The Church of the Good Shepherd has always been used for the same purpose. Can you think of any reason why a church like this would ever change?

Bullocks Wilshire

Church of the Good Shepherd

Restoration

Both of the buildings on these two pages are made in distinctive architectural styles that were very popular in the 1920s and 1930s.

- Why do you think that the Bullocks Wilshire building was left empty and not demolished when the shops were not used any more? Why do you think the law college was not built in a new building?
- Are there any buildings in your local area that have remained unchanged? If so, why do you think they have stayed the same?
- Why do you think some buildings are kept and others are demolished? Who decides what should happen to an old building?

Investigate

Find out about an old building in your local area. How was this building used in the past? Will it be used in the same way in the future? Why might it change? Could it be used for a different purpose? How would the building need to be changed inside?

Imagine that you can travel a hundred years into the future. Write a newspaper article about the building you have chosen, explaining what it is like inside and outside, how it is used now and how it was used in the past.

Bullocks Wilshire

Church of the Good Shepherd

On the map

This map shows where the places photographed in the book are in Los Angeles.

1 Angel's Flight (pages 10, 11)
2 Beverly Wilshire Hotel (page 19)
3 Biltmore Hotel (pages 10, 11)
4 Broadway (pages 24, 25)
5 Bullocks Wilshire (pages 28, 29)
6 Cahuenga Pass (pages 8, 9)
7 Chinatown (pages 12, 13)
8 Chinese Theater (pages 14, 15)
9 Church of the Good Shepherd
   (pages 28, 29)
10 Disneyland (page 4)
11 Gower Street (page 9)
12 Hollywood (pages 6, 7)
13 Hollywood Boulevard
   (pages 24, 25)
14 Otis Art Institute (pages 26, 27)
15 Santa Monica (pages 20, 21
16 Shrine Auditorium (pages 26, 27)
17 Sunset Boulevard (pages 16, 17)
18 Witch's House (pages 18, 19)

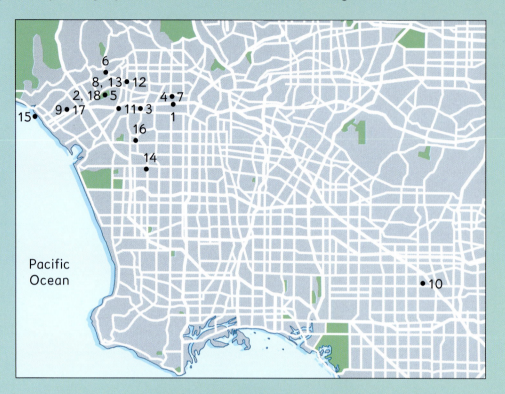

At the movies

There have been lots of movies set in Los Angeles. To get a glimpse of life in Los Angeles, watch:

Rebel Without a Cause.
Directed by Nichols Ray, 1955.

Singin' in the Rain.
Directed by Stanley Donan and Gene Kelly, 1952.

Stand and Deliver.
Directed by Ramón Menéndez, 1987.

Sunset Boulevard.
Directed by Billy Wilder, 1950.

Who Framed Roger Rabbit?
Directed by Robert Zemeckis, 1988.

On the Internet

Find out more about what tourists can do and see in Los Angeles:
www.latourist.com

Photos of famous places in Los Angeles:
www.usc.edu/isd/archives/la/historic/

A set of old picture postcards showing buildings in Los Angeles:
www.echopark.net/postcards/dt1.htm

Find out more about Chinatown:
www.chinatownla.com/

Find out more about the Chinese Theater:
www.manntheatres.com/chinese/

Find out more about the film studios:
www.seeing-stars.com/Studios/

advantage something useful or good

architect person who designs buildings

Babylonian relating to Babylon, an ancient civilization in Iraq

bequeath to leave possessions and money to others after a person has died

commercial relating to trade

cosmetics make-up

demolish to pull down or destroy

disadvantage something inconvenient or bad

drought period of no rain

freeway large road. It is the same as a motorway in Britain

Gold Rush period in the 1840s and 1850s when many people went to California to look for gold

groceries household shopping such as food and cleaning products

leisure time time spent enjoying yourself

livestock cattle and other animals kept on a farm

location real place (where a film is shot)

pier a structure built into the sea to form or protect a harbour. It is also used as a walkway and a landing place for boats

refurbish to brighten up the inside of a building by redecorating it

security firms businesses which provide protection from crime

set specially built scene or building for shooting a film

settlement a place or region where people have recently moved to set up their homes

studio building where a film is made or edited

supermarket a large shop where people can go to buy groceries and other household goods

swamp an area of soft and permanently wet ground

tepee native American tent

transport way of moving goods and people around

INDEX